Seasons of the Mind

Miriam Levine

Presentation by *BookLeaf Publishing*

Web: www.bookleafpub.com

E-mail: info@bookleafpub.com

ISBN: 9789357618090

First edition 2022

PREFACE

Poetic license does not only include the author, it extends to the reader as well. Feel free to interpret the writings here through your own experiences and make them your own.

Untitled

Because of all the things that try

To block the things I set my eye

On, and for the good of lasting greats

The show will show for goodness sakes

Faith

2

Before you find a slower path

Try just once more

Drink it slowly, take your time

Don't let it take you over

Shelter

I want to live in my memories

Rest where I feel calm

Find the beautiful moments

Stay as long as I need

At the End of the Day

I breath in through hope

And out through tears

Straining out fleeting thoughts

Marking my memory

Untitled

Only those privileged to be blind

See the darkness

And only those who are deaf

Hear the silence

Moonlight Wakes Me

6

Now I'm up and it's too late

Wishing I could be that kind of person

Who slept like a peaceful baby

Only I twitch and I'm awake again

9/11

Should've said a little prayer

Took some thought to bring the peace

If you never lived through it

It's hard to feel for it

Exhaustion

I should be tired

Overturning swelling responses

And I am so

Though it don't seem so

Chance

It comes so fast

And leaves faster

I didn't follow it

Now I lost it

Acceptance

10

I tried too many times

To like the things I ought to

Hoped to get used to

Decided it's no use

Thin Air

The feeling I crave

Is the feeling I had

But it left me

With only memories

Untitled

Empty nesters fall in love

Shower praise upon the soul

Slather oil on flaking skin

Light the fire that warms the coal

Needs never met more than a thimble

Tasting the syrupy sweetness of comfort

Parched soul always thirsting for more

Trying again but forever hurt

Wont You Help Me

Let's go on a journey

Down this long dusty road

Either it hasn't been traveled much

Or, the secret has never been told

There are no clues to follow

Just your heart and mind

Come with me and search

Maybe we will be the ones that find.

Flee

Thought that I can run away

Like everyone else does

Turns out it's a fraud

Society bought into long ago

Walk

I start it off

Pick up my feet

Crunch a leaf

Don't let eyes meet

Feel the rip

Through the holes

Dare the sun

As it rolls

Pick up the pace

Make it go

Catch the beam

Let breath flow

Challenge me

Freeze my legs

Push me hard

But no voice begs

Sayings

Why don't dry words

Curse like a curse word

Who curses in the silent parking lot,

Why don't free words

Shoot like a curse word

Who curses at the drunken enemy.

When the Day Starts

When the stars start to close

In on the night sky

And the moon fades

Into the horizon

I wrap my arms

Around the sole survivor

Who still knows the way around here

And won't lose their feet

Untitled

Candles flicker

And they envelope calm

One would think steady is the trick

But flames deny the rule

Needy

I embarrassed myself

And it's not ok

That I would try this hard

To get something I never wanted

Perception

Stranger's laughter

Fills me with angst

But children's laughter

Bubbles softly along

One a Day

These sentences are not connected. They are not
a poem. They are my thoughts on many subjects.
I have a poetic license to do this.

If my definition doesn't connect with your
disregard then don't look it up.

I'm so often in the clouds. I hardly feel the rain.

High fives are a great way to mask a slap in the
hand.

I've got so many thoughts in my head, a filing
cabinet would be nice.

Many things call my name. I hear you. I see you.
Give me time.

Thinking in rhyme makes life feel like a drama.
At least it's not reality.

Saying thoughts out loud is a solitary invasion of
privacy